Who in the World Was the UNREADY KING?

The Story of Ethelred

by Connie Clark
Illustrations by Jed Mickle

Peace Hill Press
Charles City, VA
Books for the Well-Trained Mind

Publisher's Cataloging-in-Publication Data
(Provided by Quality Books, Inc.)

Clark, Connie, 1961–
Who in the world was the unready king? : the story of
Ethelred / by Connie Clark ; illustrated by Jed Mickle.
p. cm.
Includes index.

SUMMARY:

The story of how Ethelred II became a boy-king at 10
years old, and how, because of the Vikings, he was the
last Anglo-Saxon king of Britain.

Audience: Ages 5-12.

LCCN 2004112539
ISBN 0-9728603-7-1

1. Ethelred II, King of England, 968?–1016 — Juvenile literature.
2. Great Britain — Kings and rulers — Biography — Juvenile literature.
3. Anglo-Saxons — Kings and rulers — Biography — Juvenile literature.
[1. Ethelred II, King of England, 968?–1016.
2. Kings, queens, rulers, etc.
3. Anglo-Saxons.]
I. Mickle, Jed.
II. Title.

DA154.7.C53 2005   942.01'74'092
QBI04-800103

This *Who in the World?* reader complements *The Story of the World, Vol. 2: The Middle Ages* (ISBN 0-9714129-3-6), also published by Peace Hill Press.

Peace Hill Press is an independent publisher creating high-quality educational books. Our award-winning resources—in history, reading, and grammar—are used by parents, teachers, libraries, and schools that want their students to be passionate about learning. For more about us, please visit our website, www.peacehillpress.com.

Table of Contents

Chapter 1: Boy King   1

Chapter 2: A King's Job   9

Chapter 3: The Vikings   17

Chapter 4: Emma and the Normans   27

Chapter 5: Bad Days   33

Chapter 6: The Viking King of England   39

Epilogue   45

Author's Note   46

Bibliography   47

Index   48

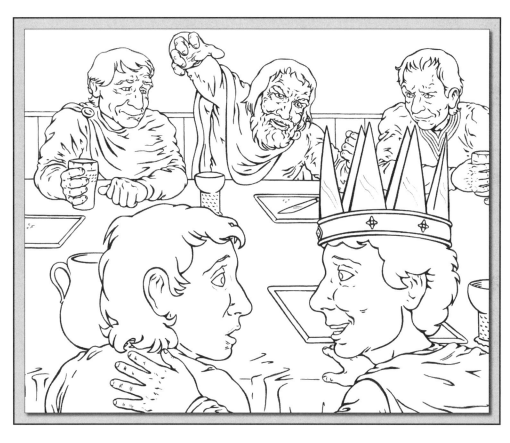

A tall, blond warrior wearing a strange horned helmet stood over him, his angry face lit by the fire.

CHAPTER 1

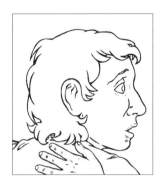

BOY KING

Ethelred stared at the crown. It was solid gold and dotted with red and purple jewels. He'd never seen anything like it, but as he stood before the fire in the great hall of the castle, a terrible thing happened. The crown slipped from his fingers and into the flames below.

A tall, blond warrior wearing a strange horned helmet stood over him, his angry face lit by the fire.

"You dropped it! That crown was worth millions. You owe me, Boy King."

"But I'm not the king," Ethelred pleaded. "Where will I get that kind of money?"

The warrior sneered. "You're the king of England. You can do anything you want."

"I'm not the king," Ethelred repeated. "I'm only ten years old!"

Ethelred awoke suddenly, covered in sweat and breathing hard. He looked around. He wasn't in the great hall. He was in his own room. It was very dark, but Ethelred could see that there was no angry warrior standing over him. No fireplace. No gold crown.

Of course, he thought. It was only a dream.

"I should be used to it by now," he muttered. After all, he'd had that same dream many times before.

Ethelred shivered as the cold March wind blew through the window, a simple slit in the earthen wall. It had snuffed out all the candles in his room hours ago. As Ethelred settled back under the covers, he couldn't stop thinking about the dream.

"I'm not the king," Ethelred said in a loud voice. "I never want to be king."

Ethelred thought about kings. There were lots of them in his family. His great-great-grandfather had been such a great king that everyone called him Alfred the Great. Then there was Ethelred's father, Edgar, who had raised a huge fleet of ships and then sailed them all the way around England every spring.

But three years ago, King Edgar had died. He left behind two sons—Ethelred and his older stepbrother, Edward. Since Edward was older, he was named king.

Ethelred thought about kings.
There were lots of them in his family.

Ethelred and Edward were stepbrothers. They had the same father—King Edgar—but Ethelred had a different mother. The boys were good friends, and even though Edward was only sixteen, Ethelred thought he was a good king. Edward was fair and just, and he listened to everyone.

But not everyone liked Edward. Especially Ethelred's mother. She was furious when Edward was crowned, because she felt that Ethelred should have been king.

She secretly plotted against Edward. She told his advisors to ignore him. And she tried to bully him into passing laws she wanted for herself.

Ethelred had always been glad that it was Edward who sat on the throne. He felt sorry for his older stepbrother, who spent most of his days in meetings with bishops and other important men called earls (*urls*). They spent hours discussing things like taxes and laws. It all sounded very dull.

Ethelred, on the other hand, spent his days outside. He practiced archery, rode his horse, and explored the forest. In the evenings he feasted with Edward and the royal court, listening to warriors tell tales of glory. His favorite was Byrhtnoth (*BURT-noth*), the white-haired earl who told about Ethelred's great-great grandfather Alfred.

"The enemy Danes conquered our land," Byrhtnoth said. "King Alfred hid in the marshes and made battle plans. Then he led his men against the Danes and won back our land."

In the evenings he feasted with Edward and the royal court, listening to warriors tell tales of glory.

Ethelred smiled as he remembered Byrhtnoth's stories. Then he remembered how cold he was. Dragging an itchy wool blanket over his shoulder, he got up and walked through the darkness to the great hall.

Normally at this hour the hall was full of servants or visitors sleeping by the fire. But tonight it was empty except for the long wooden feasting table and the fire pit in the center of the room. All that was left of the fire were a few glowing embers, and Ethelred thought crossly of the servant who had let the fire go out.

There was a strange silence about the hall. But as Ethelred poked at the fire with a stick, he heard shouting. He turned, and several people burst into the room.

Ethelred could see the tall thin figure of his mother and the short, stumpy outline of an earl. He didn't know the others. They were arguing and hadn't noticed Ethelred.

"But ma'am, we must have a proper king's funeral," the earl begged.

"If I had wanted him buried I would have ordered that when I told them to kill the brat." His mother stopped when she saw Ethelred.

The earl turned. "Uh, my lord," he stammered. "We, ah—didn't see you there."

Ethelred's mother stepped in front of the earl. "Leave us," she ordered. Ethelred began to follow the others, but he felt a cold hand on his shoulder.

"If I had wanted him buried I would have ordered
that when I told them to kill the brat."

7

He raised his eyes to his mother. She looked like a ghost in the dim firelight.

"Prepare yourself," she whispered. "Next month you will be crowned king."

Ethelred stared at her. "I beg your pardon, ma'am?"

His mother turned to go. "King," she said loudly. "You are the rightful king."

"But Edward is the king," he said.

"Edward is dead," his mother replied. "You are the king."

CHAPTER 2

A KING'S JOB

Ethelred couldn't have heard correctly. His stepbrother, Edward? Dead? He wanted to say something—anything— as if that would wake him up from what must surely be another dream. "But—" was all he could say.

"Stop standing around, boy," his mother interrupted. "You have much to do before you are crowned next month." She swept out of the room.

Ethelred stared after her.

It couldn't be true. Edward could not be dead. His mother must have made a mistake. Edward had been visiting Ethelred and his mother here at Corfe Castle. The boys had practiced archery together just this morning.

Ethelred didn't know how long he stood at the door staring after his mother. What had she been saying? "…when I told them to kill the brat."

Ethelred couldn't stop thinking about his brother. He thought about Edward on the journey to London. He thought about Edward as he and the royal court walked in a parade to Kingston-on-Thames, the place where he was to be crowned king. When it was time for the crowning ceremony, Ethelred was still thinking about Edward.

Ethelred was used to long ceremonies. But this crowning went longer than anything he could remember. The monks chanted endless songs. They said more prayers than Ethelred could count.

"Do you accept Ethelred as your king?" the archbishop asked the crowd.

"*Vivat! Vivat!*"[1] the crowd shouted in answer, but Ethelred wasn't listening.

The ceremony dragged on. Ethelred knelt before the archbishop. His mother stood behind him. The archbishop smeared holy oil on Ethelred's head, shoulders and hands.

He gave Ethelred a heavy sword and placed a gold crown on his head. The crown was too big—it fell over his eyes, and Ethelred almost dropped the sword on the archbishop's foot as he turned to face the cheering crowd.

---

1 Vivat: (*VEE-vat*) a Latin word meaning "long life." It is used as a kind of salute, or to applaud or approve someone. A similar greeting today would be "Long live the King!"

The crown was too big—it fell over his eyes,
and Ethelred almost dropped the sword.

At the great feast that afternoon, Ethelred couldn't eat. He was thinking about Edward. Someone slipped onto the bench next to him.

"I see you have not touched your dinner," his mother said. "All this food—cooked chicken, goose, duck—and you sit here thinking about it."

Ethelred choked on his mead wine. "I have a lot to think about," he muttered.

"You are ten years old," she continued. "A boy king. There is nothing for you to think about. I shall do all the thinking for you."

Boy king. Where had Ethelred heard that before? Of course. It had been in the dream. Right now his mother looked strangely like the fierce warrior in Ethelred's dream.

Ethelred was tired. He wanted to go to bed. More than anything he wanted to run out of the hall and never come back. But his mother glared at him and Ethelred knew he couldn't leave.

So he stayed long past midnight, pinching his elbows to keep himself awake. No one noticed when he finally fell asleep on the floor beneath the table.

A servant awoke him the next morning. "Hurry, sir, you are late for the meeting."

Ethelred rubbed his eyes and dragged himself to his brother's old throne, where his mother was arguing with some bishops and earls. They hardly noticed Ethelred.

*More than anything he wanted to run
out of the hall and never come back.*

"Sign these," his mother ordered, thrusting some rolls of parchment toward him. She returned to her argument. Ethelred had no idea what he was signing, but he put his feather quill to the scroll and signed.

The days dragged by. Ethelred spent them all in meetings. Everyone told him what to do, but no one gave him more orders than his mother. What was worse, everyone seemed to understand that she had ordered Edward's death. And no one seemed troubled by this fact, except Ethelred.

The long days turned into years and still Ethelred sat in meetings. But they weren't all dull. In one meeting, he learned that his face would appear on English money.

England made the finest coins in the world at the time. They were small silver coins called pence that were worth about a penny. Five pence would buy a sheep, and ten pence would buy a pig. To buy a few loaves of bread and some vegetables to eat, you could easily break a pence in half with your thumb to make "half-pence."

Ethelred liked seeing his picture on the coins, but he still thought about his brother, and decided to have coins made with Edward's picture, too.

The silver coins were beautiful and plentiful because England was a wealthy country. Everyone in Europe talked about England's wealth. Everyone envied England's riches. Everyone, including the Vikings.

The Vikings were back.

CHAPTER 3

THE VIKINGS

A few years after Ethelred became king, he got some bad news. The Vikings were back.

The Vikings were fierce warriors from Denmark, Norway, and Sweden. They had heard about England's great silver coins and wanted to get some for themselves. But now they wanted even more. They wanted England's greatest treasure—her land.

At first, the Vikings cruised up and down the English coastline in their powerful longboats, searching for unguarded treasure. The easiest targets were monasteries. These were places of learning where monks lived quietly and peacefully.

The Vikings would jump out of their longboats and attack the monasteries by surprise. They stole gold, precious cloth, and jewelry. Then they destroyed the buildings and killed or kidnapped the monks.

Lately the Vikings had grown bolder. They attacked entire cities! Sometimes the English were able to fight back. Ethelred's old, white-haired warrior friend Byrhtnoth was leading the battle against the Vikings.

One August evening in the year 991, Ethelred, who was now a grown man, stood alone before the fire pit in the great hall. Even though it was summer, the castle walls were damp and he needed warmth.

"Ahem," someone coughed. Ethelred realized that he was not alone. One of his earls stood near him. Ethelred returned to his throne and sat down.

"What is it?"

The earl coughed again. "Your friend, sir, earl Byrhtnoth."

"Yes? What about him?"

"There was a battle, sir," he explained. "The Vikings landed at a place called Maldon. Byrhtnoth and his men blocked them from crossing a bridge. The Vikings demanded money and treasure, sir, but Byrhtnoth would not give it to them. He said he would rather stand and fight."

Ethelred listened as the earl continued. "He fought well, sir. Even when some of his men left for fear of the Vikings, Byrhtnoth kept fighting. But the Vikings won, sir. Byrhtnoth was killed."

*"The Vikings demanded money and treasure, sir,
but Byrhtnoth would not give it to them.
He said he would rather stand and fight."*

Ethelred sat quietly for a long time. He thought about the brave, white-haired warrior who told stories of heroes. Now Byrhtnoth was a hero, too. But he had also been the strongest, most trusted warrior Ethelred had. What would Ethelred do now?

The next morning he called his bishops and earls together for advice.

"Sir, if I may make a suggestion," said one of the archbishops. "Perhaps if we simply give these Vikings money, they will stop stealing it."

Ethelred stared at the archbishop. He did not like the idea of giving money to these Viking bullies. After all, Byrhtnoth had not given them anything.

But without Byrhtnoth to lead it, England did not have an army powerful enough to fight the Vikings. Ethelred wished his stepbrother Edward were still alive. Edward would have known what to do.

Ethelred sighed. "We shall try your plan," he said to the archbishop. He ordered the earls to fill a treasure chest with silver coins, gold, and precious jewels. "Hand it over to the leader of the Vikings," he told them.

The earls brought the treasure to the Viking camp. When they returned they told Ethelred that the Viking leader had taken the money. He then boarded his longship and sailed back to Denmark.

"Perhaps if we simply give these Vikings money, they will stop stealing it."

Ethelred could hardly believe it. He celebrated with a great feast. He invited all of his earls and bishops. He thought he had rid England of the dreaded Vikings forever.

He was wrong.

The Vikings returned the next year, and this time, they attacked the city of London itself. The Londoners defended their city and the Vikings moved on. They began destroying other towns and villages.

"Perhaps we should pay the Vikings more," another archbishop suggested. "But this time, we should make them sign a treaty saying they will stop destroying everything in their path."

Ethelred shrugged. Maybe the bishop was right. Maybe it would work this time.

So Ethelred gave his earls and bishops a box filled with treasure and sent them to the Viking king. His name was Anlaf. When he received the gold and silver treasure, Anlaf promised that he would make peace with England and return to Norway.

As Anlaf sailed away, Ethelred celebrated again with his earls and bishops.

But the next year, more Vikings returned. They took back all of the lands that Ethelred's great-great grandfather, Alfred the Great, had won.

The Vikings attacked again and again. Each time, Ethelred took the advice of his earls and bishops, and offered them more money. The money always seemed to stop the Vikings for a while, but they always returned. And they were stronger each time.

As the years passed, Ethelred grew angry. He was angry with his mother for having Edward killed, even though she was long dead by now. He was furious at the earls and bishops for giving him so much advice. But his greatest rage was at the Vikings, who had bullied him for so long.

"We will fight the evil Vikings," he said one day.

The earls and bishops grew white with fear. "But sir," an earl said shakily. "We have seen their ships, sir. They appear out of nowhere, like dragons. They land in our ports, breathing fire. Then the Vikings come racing out, like monsters, sir."

"We have already given them so much of our silver," said another. "We have hardly any money left to build ships or pay soldiers."

"My father built a great fleet of ships. What has become of it?" Ethelred asked.

"Those are trading ships, sir," a bishop answered. "They are not fit for battle."

"Then we will make them battle-ready," Ethelred replied. "And we will train our men for battle, too."

The earls and bishops looked at each other. Turn regular ships into battleships? It was crazy. No ship could ever match the fast, powerful Viking longboats. Building an army would take years, and with Byrhtnoth dead, there were no great military leaders left.

Ethelred managed to scrape together a few ships, but they were old and leaky. It was a ragtag fleet and his leaders weren't much better.

The worst of them was Elfric. Earl Elfric had told Ethelred many stories about his great deeds. There was the time he had fought off ten Vikings all by himself and won. Then there was the time he had saved his village from the Vikings. So Ethelred put Elfric in charge of fighting the Vikings.

Ethelred felt better with Elfric in charge, until one evening, a messenger came to the castle. He was a boy, about twelve years old. He had news about Elfric's first battle with the Vikings.

"Well, boy, how did it go?" Ethelred asked eagerly.

"We lost many men, sir, but we defeated the Vikings."

Ethelred beamed. "I knew I had chosen a great leader in Elfric," he said.

"Elfric?" The boy looked puzzled. "Elfric left, sir."

"Left? What do you mean?"

The boy explained that Elfric never stopped telling stories about himself, even as the Viking longboat landed. But when the Vikings came tearing out of it, Elfric stopped and stared at the huge warriors as if he'd never seen them before. His face was white.

"Then he started acting funny, sir. He pretended to get sick over the side of the wall. Then he turned around and ran away. We never saw him again."

Ethelred put his face in his hands and sighed deeply. Would England ever defeat these Vikings?

**The most powerful among them was
a man named Swein Forkbeard.**

CHAPTER 4

EMMA AND THE NORMANS

Ethelred's battle leaders acted cowardly, but the Viking leaders grew stronger than ever. The most powerful among them was a man named Swein (*swane*) Forkbeard.

Forkbeard was the son of the Danish king, and he had his father's armies to help him. But he had even more help, from a warlike people who lived in France.

Normandy, an area in northern France, lay just across the English Channel. Between raids, the Vikings stopped there to rest and get supplies. Forkbeard often spent the winter there. The people who lived there, known as Normans, swore they were Ethelred's friends. But the Normans were also of Viking blood. Their ancestors had been Vikings, and they felt it was their duty to help Forkbeard and the Vikings, too.

"If I may make a suggestion," one of his bishops said one day.

Ethelred sighed. His own ideas about fighting the Vikings had been such a failure that he had started taking advice from others again.

"Yes," Ethelred said wearily. "What is your suggestion?"

"You could marry," the bishop said. "The Norman ruler has a sister. A marriage to a Norman would help you, sir."

In those days, kings didn't marry because they fell in love. They arranged weddings with brides from other lands to create special friendships, called alliances, with those kingdoms.

Ethelred had never met the sister of the Norman ruler. Emma was a teenager, and he was much older. She had never even been to England. But Ethelred needed Norman help if he was ever going to get rid of the Vikings. So he followed the bishop's advice and made an agreement with the Norman ruler to marry Emma.

On the day Emma arrived from Normandy, Ethelred sent out a huge party to greet her. There were beautiful white horses, ladies in waiting, and of course, lots of gifts. After all, Emma was going to be the new queen of England.

There was only one problem. Emma didn't speak any English.

Ethelred tried to imagine what it was like for Emma to leave her family and her country and sail across the ocean to a new home where no one spoke her language. He brought

*There were beautiful white horses,
ladies in waiting, and of course, lots of gifts.*

tutors to the castle so that she could learn English and English customs. It didn't take long for Emma to feel at home.

The Normans stopped giving shelter to the Vikings for a while, and Ethelred was happy with his young queen.

But Ethelred's problems were far from over.

One autumn day, an earl came to talk to him. Ethelred could tell by the frightened look on the earl's face that something was wrong.

"There is a plan, sir," the earl whispered.

Ethelred leaned in closer to hear. "What kind of plan?"

"A plan, sir, to trap you and slay you. And all of us, sir. So that England can be invaded."

Ethelred slammed his fist on his throne. He knew that the ringleader of the plan must be the dangerous Viking, Swein Forkbeard. He had gone too far this time. Now Forkbeard would pay.

"Bring me the other earls and bishops," Ethelred shouted.

Emma was in the great hall. She looked up. She had never seen the king so angry. "You are raging," she said. "You must calm down."

"Be quiet!" he roared.

When the earls and bishops came, Ethelred gave an order. A horrible one.

Emma put her face in her hands and cried. She understood English by now, and she understood this order all too well: Kill all of the Vikings in England.

She had never seen the king so angry.

CHAPTER 5

Bad Days

When Ethelred's great-great grandfather Alfred had driven the Danes out of his kingdom more than a hundred years earlier, he agreed that if they became baptized Christians, they could settle in the eastern part of the country. This area of England became known as the Danelaw.

The Danes were a Viking tribe, but they lived peacefully in the Danelaw. They settled down and worked as farmers. They were not like the murdering Swein Forkbeard and his men. They became friends with the Saxon peoples who lived in England.

But to Ethelred, they were still Vikings. After Ethelred gave his terrible order, hundreds of these innocent Danes were brutally murdered. This cruel attack became known as the St. Brice's Day Massacre, because it occurred on St. Brice's Day, November 13, 1002.

News of the horrible event reached Forkbeard. Now it was his turn for revenge.

For the next ten years, Forkbeard and his men angrily fought their way through England, taking entire cities by force. They demanded payment or they would destroy even more cities. Now Ethelred had no choice. He had to keep paying them more gold and silver, or they would destroy all of England.

To get money to pay the Vikings, Ethelred taxed his people. But in the year 1005 there was a terrible famine, so there was very little for anyone to eat.

One evening, well past midnight, Emma walked quietly into the great hall where Ethelred sat working.

"My lord," she said softly. "Your people are starving. They are weary. You must stop taxing them."

Ethelred continued to look at his scroll. But Emma had more to say.

"When Forkbeard enters the cities, the people do not fight him, my lord. They welcome him. They call him their king."

Ethelred looked up at her angrily.

"Where have you heard this? Who is calling him king?"

"Everyone, my lord. In all of the great cities—Oxford, Winchester, Wallingford. They will fight for him, not against him. You know that Forkbeard is headed for our castle. There is no one here who will fight against him."

"My son, Edmund Ironside, will fight," Ethelred said. This was true. Ethelred's eldest living son was a young man. He was a strong leader, too.

"But Edmund Ironside cannot raise an army strong enough to fight the Vikings," Emma said. She looked hard at Ethelred. "No soldier will fight for a king who kills his own people."

Emma had not forgiven Ethelred for killing the Danes. Ethelred put his head in his hands. He knew she was right. He had made a mess of everything. He wished he could run away, just as he'd wished he could run away the night he was crowned king so many years ago.

"I will not fight for you, either." Emma said. She turned and walked away. The next morning, she sailed for Normandy.

"You must send your younger sons away, too," an earl told Ethelred as he watched her go. "Edmund Ironside can take care of himself, but the boys are in danger here."

Ethelred once again did as he was told. He sent his younger sons, Edward and Alfred, to Normandy. An archbishop went along to protect them.

That same night, Ethelred had a dream. He was standing by the fire in the great hall of the castle, holding his crown in his hands. The crown fell into the fire, and a Viking warrior stood over him, his angry face lit by the flames.

"That crown was worth millions," he sneered. "You owe me."

"But how will I pay for it?" Ethelred asked. "My people have no more money."

"Then leave," the Viking growled. "Your people don't want you anymore. They want a new king. Leave and never come back."

When Ethelred awoke, it was Christmas morning. He got up, but he didn't celebrate. Instead, he did something no English king had ever done. He did what the Viking in his dream told him to do. He left his throne. He left England. He sailed away to Normandy.

*He left his throne. He left England.
He sailed away to Normandy.*

CHAPTER 6

THE VIKING KING OF ENGLAND

In Normandy, Ethelred stayed at his brother-in-law's castle with Emma and his two younger sons, Edward and Alfred. He stayed in bed every day. Ethelred was an old man now. And he was ill.

In the meantime, Forkbeard went to London and the king's castle. As Emma had predicted, the starving and battle-weary people welcomed him with open arms, proclaiming him king.

But one morning, a few months later, an earl awoke Ethelred. "Sir," he said. "Forkbeard has died. Your people want you to return to England."

Ethelred gave the earl a suspicious look. "Only a few months ago, they wanted Forkbeard for their king. Now they want me back. How can this be?"

The earl shrugged. "No king is dearer to the people than their own king," he said.

Perhaps the earl was right. Perhaps his people really did want Ethelred to return. So as he had always done, Ethelred did as the earl told him.

That spring, he sailed back to England. His old advisors— the bishops and earls—were surprised at how old and tired Ethelred had grown in only a few months.

They had a few more suggestions. "Rest," said the archbishop. "Go to bed, sir," said an earl.

Ethelred did as he was told.

The earls and bishops advised Ethelred as he lay sick in his bed. They told him of Edmund Ironside's victories over the Vikings.

"The Vikings still want England," the bishop said. "Forkbeard's son, Canute (*ka-NOOT*) is planning to attack the cities of Dorset, Wiltshire, and Somerset."

Ethelred nodded. It took practically all of his strength to listen.

"You will feel better soon, sir," the bishop said. "Then you shall return to the throne."

For the first time in a long time, Ethelred didn't listen to the bishop. He was thinking about the next king of England. "Bring Edmund to me," he said.

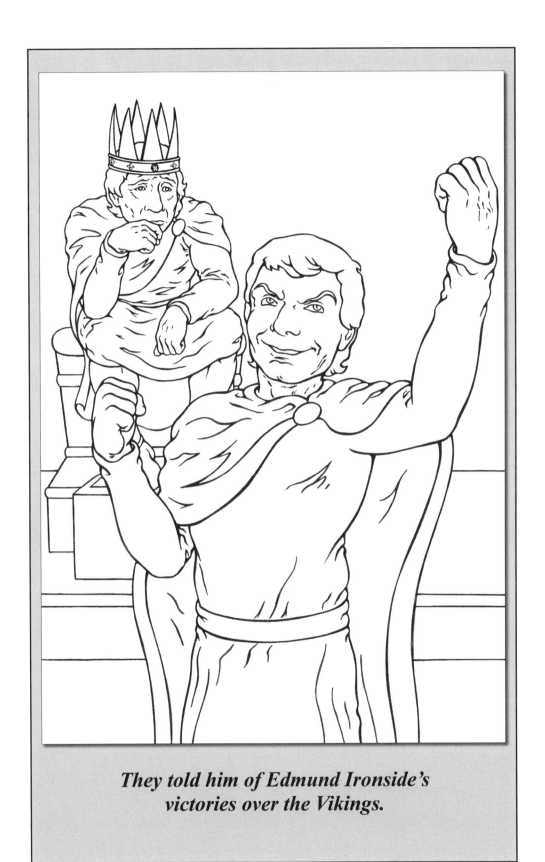

***They told him of Edmund Ironside's
victories over the Vikings.***

A few days later, Edmund stood next to his father's bed. Ethelred looked at him through tired eyes. "You will be a better king than I could ever be," he whispered feebly.

It was the last thing he said to his son. With Edmund at his bedside, Ethelred died on April 23, 1016.

A few days later, Edmund was crowned king. He didn't have a big feast because he was too busy fighting the Viking Canute. Through the spring and early summer, Edmund and his forces battled the Vikings.

But by summer's end, Edmund and Canute were tired. "It's useless," Edmund said. "Canute wins some battles, and I win others. We keep fighting, but no one wins."

The two men decided to divide England between them. But in the fall, Edmund Ironside died. Canute took over Edmund's land and became king of England.

Ethelred's terrible dreams had finally come true. Canute, the tall Viking warrior, now stood in the great hall of the castle, wearing Ethelred's golden crown. But there was no sneer on his face. Canute was a good man and a wise king. And for a time, there was peace in England again.

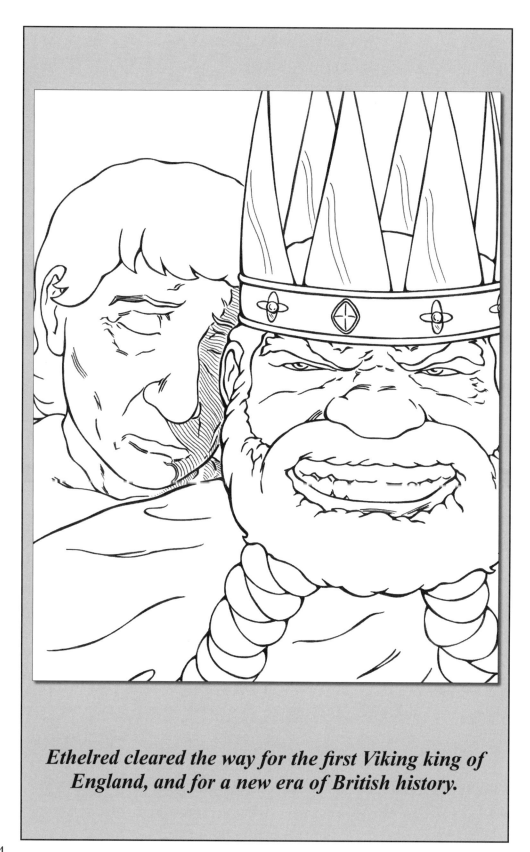

Ethelred cleared the way for the first Viking king of England, and for a new era of British history.

Epilogue:

Ethelred's story doesn't end here. After Ethelred died, people began calling him the Unready, and he's been known throughout history this way. Was this because he was too young to be king? Was he "unready" for the Viking invasions? Actually, his nickname is a word joke called a "pun."

Back in Ethelred's day, the English language was very different and Ethelred meant "good advice." "Unred" meant "bad advice." So Ethelred the Unready means something like Good Advice, Bad Advice.

It's true that Ethelred received lots of advice. But whether it was good or bad doesn't seem important now. What is important is that Ethelred never really stood up to the Vikings. And because of that, he cleared the way for the first Viking king of England, and for a new era of British history.

Author's Note:

Ethelred lived about a thousand years ago, before newspapers or books were invented. Very few people in Ethelred's day could read or write, so there is precious little written about him. Most of what we know about Ethelred comes from a very old manuscript called *The Anglo-Saxon Chronicle*. No one knows who wrote it, but it's believed the author wrote it in London a few years after Ethelred died.

Another source is *The Battle of Maldon*, a long poem about Byrhtnoth, the great white-haired warrior. We get other historical information from sermons that ministers wrote, and from archeological digs. I have used these sources to piece together the story of Ethelred. The facts of this story are true. But like others who have written about historical figures, I have used my imagination to create Ethelred's dreams and conversations. I did this to try to understand why Ethelred made his choices.

No one really knows why he let himself be bullied by the Vikings, or why he left his throne when Swein Forkbeard invaded London. Was Ethelred a coward or was he just unprepared for his job? Historians have debated questions like these for centuries. Perhaps you can add your own opinion to the debate.

BIBLIOGRAPHY

Ashdown, Margaret. *English and Norse Documents Relating to the Reign of Ethelred the Unready*. New York: Russell and Russell, 1972.

Henson, Donald. *A Guide to Late Anglo Saxon England*. Norfolk, UK: Anglo Saxon Books, 1997.

Lacey, Robert and Danziger, Danny. *The Year 1000: What Life Was Like At The Turn of The First Millennium*. New York: Little, Brown and Company, 1999.

Lawson, M.K., *Cnut, The Danes In England in the Early Eleventh Century*. London: Longman Publishers, 1993.

Richards, Julian D. *Viking Age England*, Charleston, UK: Arcadia Publishing, 2000.

Scragg. Donald, Ed. *The Battle of Maldon*. Oxford: Basil Blackwell, Ltd., 1991.

Stafford, Pauline, *Queen Emma and Queen Edith*. Oxford, Blackwell Publishers, 1997.

INDEX

(*Italicized* numbers refer to illustrations.)

Alfred (son of Ethelred) 35, 39

Alfred (the Great) *3*
Created Danelaw 33
Won land from Danes 4

Alliance 28

Anglo-Saxon Chronicle, The 46

Anlaf 22

Battle of Maldon, The 46

Byrhtnoth 6, *19,* 20, 24
In *The Battle of Maldon* 46
Killed in battle 18
Told tales 4

Canute
Became king of England 42
Planned to attack England 40

Corfe Castle 9

Danelaw 33

Danes 4, 33, 35

Edgar 2

Edmund Ironsides 35, 40-42, *41*

Edward (stepbrother of Ethelred) *3, 5,* 14, 20, 23
> Dead 8
> Ethelred's mother plotted against 4, 14, 23
> Named king 2

Edward (son of Ethelred) 35, 39

Elfric 24-25

Emma 39
> Arrived from Normandy 28-*29*
> Sailed for Normandy 35
> Told Ethelred to stop taxing his people 34
> Upset by Ethelred's order 30

England
> Danelaw as part of 33
> Ethelred left *37*
> Had much land 17
> Made the finest coins in the world 14
> Vikings destroyed cities in 34

Ethelred
> As a grown man
>> Heard of Byrhtnoth's death 18, 20
>> Left his throne 36-*37*
>> Ordered the Vikings killed 30
>> Received lots of advice 45
>> Returned to his throne 40
>> Taxed his people 34
>> Thought he had rid England of the Vikings 22
> As the boy king 12-14
> His son Edmund 35, 40-42, *41*

Ethelred's mother 4-14, *7, 11, 13,* 23

Forkbeard, Swein *26*
>Died 39
>Planned to kill Ethelred 30
>Welcomed by the English 34-39

Kingston-on-Thames 10

London
>Ethelred's journey to 10
>Forkbeard went to 39
>Vikings attacked 22

Maldon 18. *See also* Battle of Maldon, The

Normandy 27-28, 35-36-37, 39

St. Brice's Day Massacre 34

Vikings *16*
>Attacked London 22
>Attacked monasteries 18
>Envied England's wealth 14
>From Denmark, Norway, and Sweden 17
>Fought Byrhtnoth *19*
>Lost to Edmund Ironsides 40

ALSO AVAILABLE FROM PEACE HILL PRESS:

Who in the World Was the SECRETIVE PRINTER?
THE STORY OF JOHANNES GUTENBERG

by Robert Beckham
illustrations by Jed Mickle

Johannes spent his days shut away, working on a mysterious project. His neighbors wondered what he was doing in his metal shop. Why did he need so much money? Was he making expensive gold jewelry? Weapons? Armor? What project could possibly take up so many hours of Johannes' time? **What was Johannes doing behind the closed doors of his shop?**

Discover the intriguing story of Johannes Gutenberg. In this engaging

biography, Robert Beckham goes beyond the few facts children are usually told about the inventor of the printing press and tells us Gutenberg's story. What was Johannes up to? Find out, in *Who in the World Was the Secretive Printer? The Story of Johannes Gutenberg*.

ISBN 0-9728603-6-3 $9.50